"ANNIE?"

Mrs. Jones looks over the top of her glasses at Annie's desk.

"Ahem," she clears her throat and begins again, "Annie, would you care to join us this morning?"

Snickers erupt across the room, as the other students turn to look at Annie.

"Annie?" Mrs. Jones said a little more firmly, with two distinct scowl lines appearing between her brows.

Mrs. Jones believes that she will have permanent furrows carved between her brows after this year is over!

Annie Books Series© by Michelle Fattig

Experience Attention Deficits Through the Eyes of a Child

A Windy Day with Annie

A Prairie Day with Annie

Bully-Be-Gone with Annie

Viva Le Resistance!

Coming soon:

Making Friends and Keeping Them with Annie

Learning to be Nice with Annie

Stopping the Blurting Days with Annie

Managing the Distracto-Days with Annie

Calming the Stormy Days with Annie

A Prairie Day with Annie

Experience Attention Deficits
Through the Eyes of a Child

by Michelle Fattig, Ed.S.

pictures and prologue by Josh Fattig

Annie Books©

Flower by the Water Publishing Genoa, NE

www.anniebooks.com

This book is dedicated
to my wonderful husband,
amazing children,
and our family.

Text copyright © 2007 by Michelle Fattig.

Illustrations copyright © 2007 by Josh Fattig.

All rights reserved under international and Pan American
Copyright Conventions. Published in the United States by
Flower by the Water Publishing.

Library of Congress Control Number: 2007925667

Library of Congress Cataloging-in-Publication Data

Fattig, Michelle. A Prairie Day with Annie / Michelle Fattig ;
Illustrated by Josh and Lili Fattig.

"Annie Books" SUMMARY: In her own words, a young girl
describes her feelings and emotions about living with
Attention Deficits.

ISBN 978-0-9795805-1-2 (pbk)

Manufactured in the United States of America.

Michelle and Josh both have
Asperger's Syndrome
and Attention Deficit Disorders.
They use their unique insight
and experience to fight crime, battle evil,
promote world peace,
and to create this humorous,
yet meaningful story of a child
experiencing the challenges of
Asperger's Syndrome or ADD.

Prologue
Annie's Gift

Once, a long time ago, there was a young, poor girl named Annie.

She lived with her many relatives in a small, dirty farm outside of town.

Annie's father had been killed in the Great War, so her grandfather cared for the family.

Her grandfather was a stern, sad man, and he always made sure each of his grandchildren did their part to help keep the family from starving.

Annie's brothers and sisters each had well-developed talents that made them useful on the farm.

Their gifts were: strength, wisdom, and agility.

As she grew older, Annie became more and more aware of her siblings' qualities.

She began to believe that she had no talents, and would be useless to her grandfather.

She became very sad and lonely.

It was one cold autumn day, when her grandfather asked her to retrieve some books from the dusty attic, that she discovered her true talent.

As she fumbled her way through the cobweb-filled darkness, she spotted an ominous-looking shape that was hidden by a sheet.

Curiosity seemed to tug at her clothes; it compelled her to peer under the sheet.

She lifted the sheet a little, and could only see shadows.

Annie pulled the sheet off with one sharp yank, giving rise to an enormous cloud of dust that threatened to suffocate her.

When the smoke cleared, her eyes gazed upon a magnificent piano.

Never had Annie laid eyes upon something so massively beautiful.

She ran her hand along the sleek, black bench, which sat in front of the piano.

Without noticing, Annie sat down on the bench, her hands lifted the heavy cover off of the keys.

The brilliant contrast of the ivory keys to the coal-black body was enough to make Annie forget the woes that her family caused her.

She struck a note; not believing the piano could sound any more breathtaking than it looked.

A soft tone cut the deadly silence of the attic, seeming to blow the dust off the walls and floor with its intensity.

The sound seemed to float from the back of Annie's mind, holding her in a trance from which she never wanted to awaken.

Before she knew what she was doing, her hands began to glide from key to key with the swiftness of a sparrow.

She couldn't believe that her hands could have created such beautiful sounds.

Her music flowed like the sound of water running through the rocks of the Waal River, and she knew it.

This made her even more intensely happy than before.

The girl played and played until her hands became numb, but still she played, growing faster, until the feverish heat surrounding her consumed her.

The room began to fade away from her.

She slowed down as a hand briskly grabbed her, and dragged her from her dream world.

At first, Annie thought she was imagining the hand, and she fought to shrug it off, but the hand remained firmly clasped on her shoulder.

She looked up, and found her grandfather's cold, gray eyes gazing down upon her, with a look she'd never seen before—it was a look of stunned admiration.

"You've found it," was the only thing her grandfather could choke out.

Annie's grandfather became quite fond of her gift.

He purchased many records: Mozart's *Turkish March*, Beethoven's *Fur Elise,* and many of Bach's minuets for her to listen to and try to emulate.

This, of course, didn't help them financially.

Soon Annie became a virtuoso, a master of her art.

Her friends tried to persuade her to write her music down and sell it, but she could not read the frustrating notes, let alone write them.

Annie's grandfather had heard tell of a man who lived in a nearby town, who boasted that he was the greatest pianist north of the southern pole.

He made a claim that if a young pianist could best him at his art, he would pay her 30 gold marks.

Intrigued by the offer of money, Annie's grandfather told the man to be ready for his granddaughter at 3:00 in his theater the next day.

When Annie heard the news, she was terrified.

She, too had heard of this great musician, and that he prided himself on destroying his competitors' dreams of greatness.

Still, she wanted to make money for her family.

When 3:00 rolled up the next day, Annie and her family walked in from the dusty streets.

Immediately, above the dark, silhouetted crowd, Annie spotted a figure bent over the keys of a dusty black piano.

He wore a loose, velvety jacket that fanned out at the wrists, hiding his hands.

His hair was long and ragged, and it hung over his face, as he played furiously on the faded keys.

The massive crowd gasped and cheered as the figure poured out his music, with a demented expression that looked frightening.

Annie noticed how the figure played, as if the very spirit of the music he was creating possessed him.

As if he sensed them walk in, the man stopped, stood up, and stepped back from the piano, his subtle sneer daring Annie to play, accompanied by the roar of the crowd.

Annie hesitantly sat on the bench,
gazing one last time at the man before
settling her hands on the keys.

The fear began to creep up through her gut, as she realized how many people were watching her.

She forced her fear to the side, as she played her first note.

The man looked at Annie and chuckled softly.

Determined to extinguish the man's arrogance, Annie began to play her own music, which became faster and faster, more intense with every note.

Her eyes closed, and she drifted away, into her dream again, throwing her thoughts into the piano like coal into a fire, fueling the devilishly mesmerizing sounds.

After what seemed like an eternity, Annie opened her eyes to a silent theater.

She slowly turned to the audience, unsure if she was dreaming or not.

At last, a man stood in the front row, clapping faster and faster.

Soon, others joined him, until the theater was filled with the thunderous roar of approval.

Stunned, Annie watched as the 30 gold marks were dropped into her hands.

Annie looked into the eyes of the man who had just sneered at her, and spotted the faintest ghost of a smile creeping slowly across his face.

"Not bad, girl, not bad at all."

"Annie!"

What? Oh, dear.

Mr. Merle said a little more firmly, "Annie, we're here!"

The kids snickered, as they were getting off the bus, pushing and shoving their way to the front.

Annie, still slouched down in her 'thinking' position, hadn't moved.

"Annie?"

What? Oh yes.

"Sorry Mr. Merle," Annie said, quickly reaching over to grab her books and jacket, "Have a good day. I'll see you tonight!"

She flounced down the stairs and headed to the school.

Mr. Merle shook his head bemusedly, "That girl really could sit happily in her own little world forever."

Mr. Merle closed the big, heavy door behind Annie, the last off as usual, and pulled slowly away.

Chapter One

Mrs. Jones and the Daily Ritual

"Jimmy?"

"Here."

"Joanna?"

"Here."

"Annie?"

"Annie?"

"ANNN-IE?"

Mrs. Jones looks over the top of her glasses at Annie's desk.

"Ahem," she clears her throat and begins again, "Annie, would you care to join us this morning?"

1

Snickers erupt across the room, as the other students turn to look at Annie.

"Annie?" Mrs. Jones said a little more firmly, with two distinct scowl lines appearing between her brows.

Mrs. Jones believes that she will have permanent furrows carved between her brows after this year is over!

"There," Annie thinks to herself, neatly folding her paper and putting her pencil carefully at the top of her desk.

Pleased that she remembered to sign her paper this time, Annie gave a self-satisfied sigh and a decisive nod.

Mrs. Jones' chiding voice chanted disapprovingly in her mind, "Now Annie, how many times have I told you? If you don't put your name on your papers, you will not get credit for your work."

"Well at least THIS time she would," Annie thought to herself.

A loud RAP on Mrs. Jones' desk interrupted Annie's thoughts.

Startled, Annie jumped in her seat and looked around the class.

Everyone was staring at her!

"Annie! Honestly!" Mrs. Jones harrumphed.

Bewildered, and confused, as the pleased expression hasn't quite left her face, Annie asks, "Honestly what?"

The classroom breaks out in laughter.

"Sit out in the hall until I can *deal* with you!" Mrs. Jones put a nasally, sneering emphasis on the "deal" part of her command.

Mrs. Jones glares balefully at the rest of the students.

"Settle down," she barks.

"But..." Annie simpers.

"Now!" Mrs. Jones chides, without looking at Annie.

Deflated, Annie glanced up through her bangs around the desks.

A few of her friends gave encouraging, but pitying glances.

Others looked on with open delight.

"Nice."

"Way to go doof."

"ADD A*nn*-ie, ADD A*nn*-ie, ADD A*nn*-ie."

Muffled comments followed her out of the room.

This is not an unusual start to the day for Annie and Mrs. Jones.

It had practically become a ritual.

Annie was just *sure* that today would be different, what with remembering her name on the paper and all.

"Why can't I just pay attention? Why can't I just pay attention? Why can't I just pay attention? Why can't I just pay attention? Why can't I just …," Annie chants to herself quietly as she struggles to keep the tears at bay.

Closing the door behind her, Annie slumps quietly to the floor.

The cracks in the ceiling are still there, where she mentally traced them yesterday.

Looking around, the crayon marks on the wall; up high, sort of hiding behind the door are still there, where she saw them yesterday, and the day before, and…no wait, the day before that was Sunday.

5

"I wonder if they had crayons when Mrs. Jones went to school," Annie muses silently to herself.

"I bet they didn't have crayons."

"I bet they didn't even have pens and pencils."

"I wonder if Mrs. Jones had to use one of the quill and ink pens they talked about in the story mom read to me last night."

"I wonder if Mrs. Jones had to ride in a wagon or even walk to school."

Hmmm…Annie's imagination began to kick in.

"I wonder if ……

Annie is standing next to an old-fashion pump.   She is wearing a flowery dress that doesn't quite reach her ankles.

The cotton skirt is blowing wildly about her legs.

The heavy woolen socks itch when she moves, and clunky, brown boots, laced up above her ankles, are stiff and uncomfortable. The boots are too tight, but she knows another pair won't be purchased until school starts again in the fall.

"Better get used to it," Annie thinks, as she subconsciously curls her toes under. During the summer she goes shoe-less, so the tight boots won't be a problem.

Her schoolmistress won't allow students in class without, "Prau-pau foot-weah."

Annie giggles to herself as she thinks of the haughty Miss, with a voice that sounds so different from anyone Annie has ever heard.

"She came on a wagon from back East," she had heard her ma and pa whispering after they thought Annie asleep.

Annie thought her ma sounded impressed at the idea of coming from, "Back East."

Annie has a bonnet tied loosely around her neck, but it is hanging limply across her shoulders, instead of tied protectively on her head, as mamma is always reminding her!

"A lady must protect her delicate skin from this blistering sun," ma says.

"When I was a girl," ma would go on, "we had enough sense to stay out of the sun."

At that, ma would always nod her head firmly, and go back to whatever task was at hand.

Annie reached for the pump handle.

"We are very lucky to have a pump," ma always tells her.

"So many still have to gather water from the creek or from rain barrels," ma has said.

If they gather water from the rain barrels, wouldn't it be gooky and brackish? Annie wonders, as she pulls the handle up with both hands, lifting it above her head, stepping underneath, and completing the motion like a weightlifter thrusting the weighted bar high above his head triumphantly.

Do they scoop up minnows or algae with the buckets when they gather water from the creek, she further ponders?

Would the algae get stuck in your teeth?

Annie keeps a tight hold on the pump handle as she steps around to the side of it.

She doesn't need to keep a hold of the handle; it stays up all by itself. But Annie is a creature of habit, and distractedly continues about her task.

Maybe the minnows would get in your mouth and wiggle around some.

"I wonder what a minnow tastes like," Annie murmurs quietly to herself.

Would it be salty?

Using all of her weight, she holds the handle with both hands. Annie drops down to a squatting position pulling the handle down with all of her might.

As the handle comes down, Annie deftly steps out and away, coming back over the top of the bar, and pushing down like a gymnast might on the uneven parallel bars.

10

Nothing.

No water.

"Shoot!" Annie exclaims looking around sheepishly.

Ma says Annie should mind herself and speak only as a lady might speak.

Starting again, Annie assumes the position with both hands pulling upwards on the handle.

After a few failed attempts, Annie succeeds in priming the pump.

Priming the pump helps get the water started.

With aching arms, Annie raises and lowers the handle in a rhythmic motion producing, at first, a spurt and then a trickle of water with each stroke.

The pump creaks, squeaks, and groans with each repetition.

"I know it would be slimy," Annie thinks, still contemplating the minnows.

More rapidly now, Annie is pushing the handle up and down, stretching high then bending low at the waist with each repetition.

"Annie."

"Annie!" Ma is calling for her.

Annie looks down at the bucket, only half full.

Annie's shoes, however, are MORE than half full.

Annie had forgotten to secure the round handle of the bucket over the notch on the pump.

Only a small amount of the stream was hitting the bucket.

The rest was hitting Annie!

She will have to tread to school, with the slurping, squishing sound wet boot leather makes when you walk.

Her feet will be all shriveled, like someone who spent too much time in the swimming hole, when she takes them off tonight.

"Oh dear," a much more ladylike exclamation, Annie thinks.

Ma would be proud…

Chapter Two
Crayon Marks, Ceiling Cracks, and a Wad of Gum

A hand on her shoulder interrupts Annie.

"Annie," Mrs. Jones repeats exasperated, "I have been calling for you to come back to class."

Shaking her head, Annie looks around…same crayon marks on the wall, same cracks in the ceiling, same gum stuck under the door handle, no wait…there was no gum there yesterday.

Was there gum there yesterday?

"I didn't see gum there yesterday," Annie murmurs.

It could have been there yesterday.

"Annnn-IE," more sternly this time.

"Oh, sorry Mrs. Jones!" Annie blurts out, as she jumps to her feet.

Dusting herself off, Annie glances up to Mrs. Jones.

"Mrs. Jones?" Annie ventures.

"Mmm, yes Annie," Mrs. Jones replies distractedly, trying to keep an eye on the class, as she waits for Annie to straighten herself.

"Mrs. Jones, what do you think a minnow tastes like?" Annie asks, looking brightly up at her teacher.

"Wh-what? What do you mean, what do I think a minnow tastes like?!

"Honestly Annie!

15

"Did you spend any time thinking about WHY you were sitting out in the hallway?" Mrs. Jones looks positively apoplectic.

Apoplectic. Annie likes that word.

Last week, when mom made her stay in her room after getting the letter from Mrs. Jones about how the day went, Annie had looked through the A's in the dictionary.

One must figure out how to spend time in a constructive manner, when one is frequently banished to one's room.

Apoplectic had popped out at Annie.

Apoplectic…at rest, becalmed, dead, deadlocked, deathly, firm, fixed, frozen, halted, immobile, immotile, inanimate, inert, lifeless, numb, palsied, paralyzed, petrified, quiescent, quiet, spellbound, stable, stagnant, stalled, standing, static, stationary, steadfast, still, stock-still, torpid, transfixed, unmovable, unmoved, unmoving.

What a simply MARVELOUS WORD!

Wait, what does torpid mean?

A blank stare was the only response from Annie to Mrs. Jones' question.

Annie was still rolling the words around on her tongue, oblivious to the storm brewing in Mrs. Jones.

"Let's use this as a *teaching moment.*" Mrs. Jones has that 'hands on hips, bending slightly at the waist, earnest expression' she frequently gets when speaking with Annie.

Annie looks back expectantly.

"Well…" prompts Mrs. Jones without changing posture.

Annie looks at her feet and shuffles a toe at a wadded up piece of writing paper. She hadn't noticed the writing paper before.

It is a lined paper with writing visible.

What was written on it?

Was it a note?

Maybe it was a note from Dougie to Annie, expressing his undying love.

Dougie sits behind Annie. He has reddish brown hair that sticks out of his head at all angles. He has freckles and one of the biggest smiles Annie has ever seen.

"I wonder if Dougie would have liked living on the prairie…"

Annie's imagination is at it again.

Skipping brightly in the morning sunshine, Annie swings a pail in a great arcing motion.

Her long dark braids trail down her back and her bonnet still lies loosely about her shoulders.

The pail is small and gray.

The little handle feels cool in her hand.

Ma has tucked biscuits, an apple, and some jerked meat in the bottom for Annie's lunch. A checkered red and white kerchief is tucked around the food, keeping it from flies and from being crushed by Annie's careless transport.

They will pump more fresh cool water
at lunchtime.

Ma says it is so lucky that the little
school has its very own pump.

Not many schools have them you
know.

Thinking about her aching arms, Annie is not so sure that she would consider it altogether lucky!

There are very few trees about, and Annie can see far across the horizon. Tall prairie grass sways gently in the breeze.

Annie loves the feeling of the sun and breeze on her cheeks.

Ma will, of course, scold her for not covering up with her bonnet when she sees her pink cheeks!

As Annie cavorts along, she notices a boy strolling towards her.

The boy is wearing a plaid cotton shirt, and stiff looking jeans, that are slightly too short and in obvious need of mending.

Ma would never let pa out of the house in such a state.

21

The boy has stiff looking leather boots resembling Annie's very own footwear. He has dark blue suspenders and is swinging a pail along as well.

He and Annie meet up as they pass old Mr. Johnson's barn.

Old Mr. Johnson yells a lot and his dog barks constantly, but they are both actually really nice.

Neither Annie nor Dougie are afraid of Mr. Johnson's bark, or his dog's for that matter!

The boy's hair is damp and has the obvious appearance of having been "slicked down," but to no avail!

Dougie's hair would never submit to a combing, no matter how hard his ma fusses and pulls and smashes at it!

"Hey…" he begins.

Annie smiles in return.

Her grin is infectious and Dougie's eyes light up with a broad smile spreading across his face.

Dougie's teeth are kind of too large for his mouth. His teeth sort of 'take over his face' when he smiles.

"Hey…hey Annie."

That's not Dougie's voice Annie thinks.

Oops.

"Sorry Mrs. Jones," Annie says feeling sheepish.

She can tell by the expectant look on Mrs. Jones's face that she has been asked a question.

What was it? Hmm…

Oh dear..think fast…

Mmm…

Let's see…in the hallway.

Quick, quick!

"Oh why can't I just pay attention? Why can't I just pay attention? Why can't I just pay attention? Why can't I just pay attention? Why can't I just …," Annie mutters the familiar chant, as she searches desperately for a reply.

Mrs. Jones' face has the most interesting shade to it now.

It's sort of mottled reddish with little while lines around her tightly pursed mouth and interested little white indentations forming between her eyebrows.

The red color is creeping down her neck and up to her ears.

Annie thinks the coloring is really not very flattering, not very flattering at all!

"Well..." Mrs. Jones leans in toward Annie even more; her hands are now fisted on her hips.

Hmm...

Not good.

Annie studies her surroundings quickly.

Let's see, she is thinking, standing in the hallway...

Mrs. Jones seems irritated...

Mmm...

What was I supposed to be doing in the hallway?

"Going to the bathroom!" Annie

blurts loudly, clearly pleased with
herself.

"Wh-what?!" Mrs. Jones stammers.

"What…what?" Annie looks
expectantly.

This kind of confused, jumbled
exchange between the two is definitely not
new. Mrs. Jones again thinks that she will
never survive the year.

Chapter Three
To Blurt or Not to Blurt

"Oh Annie," she mutters shaking her head, "Please join the rest of the class and get out your science book. We will be talking about photosynthesis."

"Oooh, happy day! I love science!" Annie squeals silently to herself.

Taking her seat, Annie glances shyly at Dougie in his desk behind her.

"Eyes front!" Mrs. Jones commands while preparing her lesson book.

Annie knows she wasn't talking to just her, but feels chastised anyway.

Annie is used to feeling this way.

"Why can't I just pay attention? Why can't I just pay attention? Why can't I just pay attention? Why can't I just pay attention? Why can't I just ....," Annie chants to herself silently while gathering her materials.

This time I'm going to listen, she resolves.

"Okay class, let's begin. Photosynthesis is the process by which plants use energy from the sun to produce the "fuel" needed by all living things. This *conversion* is associated with the actions of the green pigment, *chlorophyll*, found in plants and trees. Most of the time, the photosynthetic process uses water and releases the oxygen that we absolutely must have to stay alive."

I'm here, I'm still listening, Annie thinks excitedly.

So far so good.

"Okay class, who can tell me what *conversion,* is?" Mrs. Jones asks emphasizing the pronunciation and looking up from her notes.

"Oooh ooh, I know this," Annie thinks as she raises her hand.

"Annie?" Mrs. Jones calls.

"Adaptation, alteration, born again, changeover, exchange, flip-flop, flux, growth, innovation, metamorphosis, modification, novelty, passage, passing, reconstruction, reformation, regeneration, remodeling, reorganization, resolution, resolving, reversal, switch, transfiguration, transformation, translation, transmutation, turning," Annie rushes out in one, almost indecipherable, breath.

Giggles and murmurs from the class.

"Oh darn, I've done it again," Annie thinks to herself, looking about abashedly.

"Why can't I just be NORMAL," she chides herself soundlessly.

"Um," Mrs. Jones drawls out, "*Yeee-ssss*. Can anyone give a more succinct answer?"

Dougie raised his hand behind Annie.

"Dougie?" Mrs. Jones prompted.

"Ch-changed?" he stammers uncertainly.

"Good Dougie," she praises, "The process *changes* unusable sunlight energy into usable chemical energy.

"Photosynthesis is the process of converting, or *changing,* light energy to chemical energy and storing it in the bonds of sugar. Photosynthesis takes place mostly in the plant's leaves, and little to none occurs in stems.

"Can anyone tell me why you think that is?" Mrs. Jones asks expectantly.

Annie raises her hand immediately.

"The parts of the leaf usually have the upper and lower epidermis, the mesophyll, the vascular bundles, and the stomates," Annie announces brightly.

Some shifting about in chairs occurs and murmurs of disbelief.

"Why…*y-e-s,* but next time, please wait for me to call on you," Mrs. Jones slowly responded, looking on disbelievingly.

Annie starts to drift to the minnows and the prairie.

"No! Not this time!" she sternly chides herself.

Focus!

"Wait. What about the algae? The algae the settlers might have scooped up in their buckets would have been green. I wonder if they drank it, if their teeth would turn green?" she chuckles silently, "NO WAIT."

"Mrs. Jones?" Annie asked, forgetting to raise her hand.

Disapprovingly, Mrs. Jones replies, "Yes?"

"Can photosynthesis happen in algae too?" Annie asked.

"Why yes, very good. It does in some forms of algae," Mrs. Jones smiled approvingly.

"Yeah me!" Annie thought.

"These epidermal cells do not have chloroplasts, so photosynthesis doesn't occur there. They actually protect the rest of the leaf.

"Can anyone tell me what a plant or tree breathes *in* and what they breathe *out?*"

Annie's hand shot up.

"I'll give you a little hint;" Mrs. Jones added after a silent pause from the class, ignoring Annie's hand now waving about somewhat frantically, "we all use it to live."

Annie leans forward in her desk using her other hand to prop her arm even higher.

"Anyone?" Mrs. Jones looks around, still ignoring Annie's frantic attempts to be called upon.

"Oxygen!" "Andy." Mrs. Jones and Annie say simultaneously.

"Annie, please. I called on Andy. Andy?"

"Oxygen." Andy states, while giving a smug sneer at Annie.

"Good Andy. Oxygen, we all need the oxygen released from the plants and trees."

The bell rings.

"That's all for today class, don't forget to read pages 22-24 in your science books," Mrs. Jones calls out as everyone tumbles out of their seats.

"Oh well. Another day is over.

That's one more day closer to summer! I guess mom will be getting the usual note," thinks Annie sighing sadly while gathering her books, papers, and jacket together.

Annie was so hoping today would be different.

While lost in thought, Annie didn't notice Dougie looking expectantly at her.

"Annie," Dougie said shyly.

"Oh! Hi!" Annie said hoping she hadn't been talking out loud to herself.

Annie was known to do that you know.

"Um, Annie," Dougie stuttered, "I really liked your answer about conversion."

What?!

He did?!

Annie looked suspiciously at his face.

Sometimes kids said nice things, but they weren't really sincere.

Annie's eyebrows shot up. He looked like he meant what he said.

"Thank you!" Annie wanted to throw her arms around him!

Dougie and Annie walked outside together.

It was a warm day with a gentle breeze. The sun shined brightly down on Dougies' dark reddish hair.

Annie squinted at him really hard. She thought she could almost see his lunch pail and suspenders.

Stop that!

"Guess I'll see you tomorrow," he said as they stopped in front of her school bus.

"Guess so," Annie replied happily.

Annie contentedly climbed the stairs of her school bus.

Settling into her seat, she threw her backpack and jacket next to her.

Annie scrunched down in the seat, bracing her knees on the seat in front of her. Settling in and wiggling to find a more comfortable position, Annie closed her eyes with a smile.

"Dougie wants to see me tomorrow," she sighed, "What a great day!"

Her thoughts drifted to a warm breezy prairie. In the distance she watched herself and Dougie walking home from school together. She smiled to herself, as she watched him reach over to take her hand.

"Stop!

"Wait!

"Hold up there!" A breathless Mrs. Jones hollers, running up to the bus.

Chapter Four
Ripping the Bandage

Mrs. Jones reaches up to grab the steel handle, located on the inner, right side partition of the school bus, while nodding a 'thank you' at the bus driver, as she hikes up the three steps into the bus. Placing her left hand on the first seat to catch her breath, she looks over the occupants of the bus for Annie.

Annie, being scrunched down and lost in thought, was oblivious.

Suddenly, she jumped at the hand on her shoulder.

"Annie," Mrs. Jones said, leaning forward and holding out a white envelope, "Did you forget something?"

An inward groan resonates through Annie, but outwardly she says, "Sorry Mrs. Jones. Thank you."

Reaching up to take the note she glances quickly to Mrs. Jones' face trying to gauge the contents.

Small tightly pursed lips with the ensuing white lines usually meant an evening alone in her room perusing the dictionary or some other modest attempt at entertainment.

A slightly distracted, smiling face equaled freedom and no scolding or disappointment from mom.

The passive, giving nothing-away face was the worst. At least the angry face allowed Annie to anticipate her fate.

Not knowing was the worst. Not being able to prepare, leaves Annie with a queasy, hollow, slightly fuzzy feeling.

Sometimes she gets that way in new situations or with new people. It's hard to feel comfortable when you don't know what to expect or how to react.

Last summer Annie and her family went to the hot springs. It was a great underground natural spring, which produced warm pools in which to swim or sit and relax. The brochure said that there would be huge, twisting water slides and lots of other great stuff!

Giddy with excitement, Annie could

barely contain herself.

Their family planned and agonized over the hours
to be endured until the big day! Finally the big day came! Leaving in the camper, it was the best day Annie could remember!

Smiling brightly with a breathless anticipation, she stared out the window all of the long hours of the trip.

Mentally she thought of the fun she would have.

Trips are good.

Trips are when everyone gets along great. Well, they get along great for the first day or so. After that, the lack of routine and regular sleep leaves everyone cranky and on edge.

"Don't think about that," she scolds

herself.

Pulling into the RV lot, dad announced, "There she is!"

Annie pressed her face tightly to the glass, glorying in the fact that they had finally arrived!

Hot springs, swimming, slides, how wonderful!

Dad pulled into the lot, paying the attendant for the amenities provided.

Annie could feel the crunch of gravel underneath the camper has they made the slow, slightly jerky turn into their parking spot.

Annie looked around at all of the people.

Just look at them all!

Look at the colorful signs and campers. Look at the big beautiful pine forest in the background.

A sinking feeling settled in the pit of her stomach.

Oh dear.

This is new.

The feeling isn't new. Oh no, of that she is very familiar!

The place is new and the people are new.

Annie's face is no longer pressed against the glass; she is now sort of shrinking back into her seat trying not to actually see out.

Annie can feel her heartbeat. She can actually feel her chest and whole body pulsate with each beat.

That can't be good.

Annie thinks she can hear the blood rushing through the veins in her brain.

As if from a distance, she hears her mom ask, "Sweetie, are you alright?"

Annie nods, but doesn't answer.

She knows what comes next as the hot tears gather behind her eyes.

"Not now. Not now. Not now," replaces her usual chant of, "Why can't I just pay attention? Why can't I just pay attention? Why can't I just ….,"

"Annie!" Mrs. Jones interrupted her revere.

"Oh, sorry?" Annie automatically replied.

"I said, to have a good afternoon," said Mrs. Jones with a bemused look and slight shake of her head.

"Only a few more weeks," Mrs. Jones thought ruefully to herself, "only a few more weeks."

Annie debated, to open...or not to open...THAT was the question!

Since Mrs. Jones' face had given nothing away, Annie could make a choice. She could agonize the entire ride home and experience *THAT* feeling, or read the note and risk mom getting mad.

Annie silently chewed her top right lip. It was an odd habit, but one that she subconsciously developed after being scolded for her incessant leg bouncing.

As long as Annie could remember she was a "leg bouncer."

No matter where she was at, no matter what she was doing, her right knee had the uncontrollable need to bounce rapidly.

Unless, of course her legs were crossed; then it was the foot dangling in the air that, almost as if having a mind of its own, beat silently in the air.

Annie's rapidly flapping foot appeared similar to a deranged humming bird in flight, so quick was the movement.

For some reason, people complained that it was distracting.

To each there own I guess!

Annie finally took a deep breath and shrugging, she tore open the envelope.

"Rip the bandage," she sighed to herself.

Better to know and face the truth, than to draw it out like the slow, painful removal of a band-aid!

"Oh dear," Annie's heart sunk.

It was the 'A' word.

The 'A' word was worse than most!

"If Annie would only APPLY herself, she would do so well," and so began Mrs. Jones' daily note to mom, "She's so bright, if only…"

The 'A' word would not only get Annie time in her room, it would also earn her a lecture from mom.

The 'A' word led to the, "Why can't you just…" lectures.

"Why can't you just try harder?

"Why can't you just get started?

"Why can't you just put something down? It doesn't have to be perfect.

"Why can't you just…."

Don't you think I would if I could?

"Why can't I just be normal? Why can't I just be normal? Why can't I just.." Annie's internal chant resounded throughout her being.

It might even earn her a lecture from dad! Dad doesn't like to get involved too often. He works a lot. He works all of the time.

"I bet if he were in the olden days he would be a very rich man with lots and lots of horses," Annie contemplates silently.

Chapter Six

Hypnotized

Pa banged noisily through the door.

CRACK!

"OOPH," a muffled explosion from pa, as his toe caught the corner of the solid, heavy table.

"Darned table," he exclaimed, quickly catching himself, and casting a guilty glance at ma.

Ma's cheeks pinkened, and she pulled a face, but said nothing as she continued stirring the pot of stew in the cast pan sitting on the cooking stove.

Pulling his weather-beaten, tan, leather hat from his head with a flourish pa bent around to plant a loud smack on ma's cheek, exclaiming, "What's to eat, woman?"

Ma continued to glare a bit, pretending to be disgruntled. But, I could tell she was pleased as her blush deepened at the kiss.

Ma likes to act stern and proper-like, but she's just covering some I expect.

Pa tried to stick his finger in the stew and ma swatted his hand away with her wooden spoon.

"Take your filthy self out to the pump you big oaf and wash up some before you try sticking your foul fingers in MY stew," ma cried indignantly.

You might think this an odd homecoming.

With that, pa scooped ma up in his big arms swinging her around and chortled, "That's the little spitfire I married, give us a big old kiss!"

Laughingly, ma smacked him again with the spoon, this time it caught him in the middle of his forehead!

Pa howled as if mortally wounded and kissed her firmly on the nose.

Pa dropped ma gently to her feet, and turned to Annie.

"There's my beautiful young-un," he grinned down at her, "How was school little one?"

"Absolutely perfect, pa," Annie beamed her reply, "I got all of my work done before anyone else. Mistress said I was a real example."

"Thatta-girl," pa bellowed!

"Annie!" ma yelled.

Why would ma be yelling?

"Annie!"

That's not ma!

Sitting up quickly, Annie looked around the bus, a little confused.

When left alone long enough with her thoughts, Annie sometimes forgets where she is or what she is doing.

Sometimes when she is reading or watching TV, she completely tunes out everything around her.

'Hypnotized' mom calls it.

"Annie," the bus driver calls out again, "Your stop!"

Luckily, Annie is the last one on the bus. She is the first to be picked up in the morning and the last to be dropped off every night.

Annie rides the bus an hour every morning and another hour every night.

At least no other kids are around to tease her about daydreaming!

"Thanks Mr. Merle," Annie smiles as she steps out, "see you in the morning!"

Mr. Merle responds, "Aiyah."

Annie doesn't know what 'Aiyah' means. But, it is the acknowledgement Mr. Merle gives her everyday to her parting salutation.

Annie starts the long walk up her drive. The driveway is almost a quarter of a mile long.

The drive is lined on either side with tall, dark, leafy trees.

When Annie was a little girl, she was terrified to make the long walk alone.

She would step from the bus, wave to Mr. Merle, wait until he was out of sight, and look both ways.

When she was sure no one was watching, Annie would grit her teeth together and *race* up the driveway, trying desperately to think of something other than the beasties that must be hiding behind each tree.

Annie would dash madly to the front door, simultaneously wrestling the knob open, while frightfully peering back to make sure nothing was coming up the path. She would FLING open the door, throw herself inside, slam the door behind her, and LOCK it, in a frantic motion.

Annie is, of course, above all of that now.

She surreptitiously glances from side to side.

Annie makes a big display of readjusting her backpack and bending to re-tie her shoe as Mr. Clover, their neighbor, drives by.

Mr. Clover gave that sort of half-hearted salute he always gives, in which he splays out his three middle fingers from the top of the steering wheel never quite relinquishing contact with the wheel and his pinkie and thumb.

Mr. Clover is an odd little man.

Without standing fully, Annie waves back at Mr. Clover.

Looking back and forth, Annie chides herself for the nervous flutter in her stomach. The trees are so big and menacing.

Even though, Annie assures herself, I'm way too old to be afraid, it wouldn't hurt me to get a little exercise.

Running is exercise.

Running is good.

Annie broke into a full out sprint as she raced up the drive.

Flying by the great line of trees, Annie looked neither right nor left. The trees became a blur.

The closer Annie got to the house, the more sheepish she felt.

Tomorrow I'll stroll casually.

Tomorrow I'll do better.

Breathing heavily from the exertion, Annie skipped the bottom two stairs, hopping onto the small landing in front of the door.

Reaching for the handle, Annie called out, "MOM!"

No immediate answer.

Pulling the screen door wide, Annie wrestled her way inside, while being accosted by Jesse.

Jesse is a 110-pound yellow-lab behemoth!

Jesse believes that it is his solemn duty as the family pet to properly greet any and all that pass the threshold of "his" home.

Laughingly, Annie fell back against the door with Jesse's front paws placed firmly on her shoulders. Annie twisted and turned her face trying to avoid the great slobbering tongue.

"Jesse!" mom's voice called out, "Get DOWN!"

Chastised, Jesse dropped to the floor. Head hanging, he had a pitiful expression.

Annie dropped to her knees, taking his giant golden head in her hands. She wrapped each hand up and behind a floppy ear, scratching gently.

"That's okay big guy," she whispered to the now contented dog, "I love you too!"

"Annie, sweetie," her mom said, "Don't take your jacket off yet, because we are going to the doctor's office."

Oh no.

Chapter Seven
No More Jell-O Please

Annie hates going to the doctor's office.

When Annie was four, she had a really bad stomachache. Although it was a really, really long time ago, she bends slightly at the waist and places her hand across her torso, reflexively.

The pain had gotten worse and worse over a few days. Annie's mom had driven her to the emergency room twice, and she had been given a thick, green, foul tasting medicine to help ease the discomfort.

The medicine was horrible and, it did little but calm the pain briefly.

Finally, Annie had been admitted to the hospital.

It was terrifying.

The walls were a pale anemic looking green and there were two beds in the room. The walls were lined with tubes, and machines that frightened the little girl in so much agony.

Mom sat on the edge of Annie's bed holding her hand tightly. A nurse bustled in holding a tray with needles, bandages, tubes, and other tools of the trade.

"Excuse me please," the nurse intoned without looking up, "Could you please step to the side? I need to set up the IV line."

Annie had no idea what an IV line was, but it did not sound good.

Annie began to shake and whimper.

"No!" She cried out as the nurse reached for her arm.

"No! No! NO!"

Annie howled and flailed, trying to keep her arms out of reach from the apparently demented nurse armed with what appeared to be a giant rubber band.

Of what a giant rubber band would be used for, Annie was unsure, but she was sure that it would not be good.

"It will be okay honey," her mother tried to soothe her, "It will be over quickly, but you have to hold still."

Hold still? Are you kidding?

A minor wrestling match ensued, with the nurse trying valiantly to pin an arm down.

Annie fought just as valiantly to avoid such a pinning.

For a four year old, Annie was pretty strong.

Abruptly, the nurse straightened, releasing the terrified girl.

"It seems that we will require assistance," she breathed out heavily, straightening her mussed hair.

"I will be back shortly," and with that, she marched resolutely through the door.

Annie can remember the feeling of intense relief like it was yesterday. She had thought the episode finished.

Within a few short minutes, the nurse returned. Behind her trailed a smaller woman carrying what appeared to be a white board with straps sticking out everywhere.

WHAT was THAT?

"A papoose board," the nurse stated to mother in response to the question Annie had not heard her utter.

The next few minutes passed in the chaos of the two nurses launching themselves at the terrified girl, wrestling her to the flat, cold, hard board and securing her to the evil contraption.

Annie struggled for all she was worth, but the two women easily subdued her. They strapped ankles, thighs, waist, arms, wrists, chest, and head to the awful board.

Traumatized, Annie called out for her mom. The nurses, however, thought it best for her mother to wait in the hallway.

The first nurse reached into her awful tray, pulling out the oversized rubber band.

"This won't hurt a bit," she said to Annie as she bent over Annie's hand.

The nurse took her time looking and patting gently, first the back of Annie's left hand, then her right. Next, the nurse looked at the crook of Annie's right arm then left, still looking, patting, and rubbing each site.

What's happening?!

Tears streamed down the sides of Annie's face. She was crying so hard it felt as if she couldn't get enough oxygen. Annie's chest heaved painfully against the cruel straps at her chest and stomach.

The nurse went back to Annie's left hand. She patted more sharply a few times, waited, and slapped at it again.

"What-are-you-doing?" A gulping breath punctuated each word as Annie struggled.

Next, the nurse took the giant rubber band, stretched it, wrapped it under Annie's wrist, pulled the ends up and away, wrapped one end over the other, and tied a loop tightly.

Annie's fingers quickly became numb.

The nurse rubbed something wet and very cold across her hand.

"This will sting a bit," she uttered while plunging a needle roughly the size of a pencil under Annie's delicate skin.

A guttural scream filled the room.

Pain stabbed through Annie.

"No! No! NO!" Annie cried over and over.

"Oh dear, it rolled," the nurse muttered as she slid the needle in and out of Annie's hand.

"We'll have to try again," Annie will never forget those awful words.

The process was repeated at her right hand, left forearm-twice, the crook of her right arm and finally her left. The needle was successfully inserted on the last try.

The nurse attached the tubing, regulated the flow, and released Annie from her bindings. She turned to tell Annie's mom that she could come back in now.

Annie, in the mean time, saw the terrifying tube disappearing into her arm. She looked up to see the frightening machine with the angrily blinking red lights and a bag of fluid hanging above it.

Annie immediately YANKED the horrible thing from her arm, at which time fluid and blood saturated her gown.

Mom walked in and screamed at the sight of Annie covered in, what appeared to be, large amounts of blood.

The nurses rushed back in, taking in the scene with a gasp.

Annie's memory is not as clear about everything that followed, but she does remember being tortured yet again and finally being taped down to the bed to keep her from pulling the IV out a second time!

Annie remembers the humiliation of rectal thermometers and of being touched and prodded. She especially remembers lukewarm, salty broth and Jell-O.

She remembers lots and lots of Jell-O.

Annie has not eaten Jell-O since she was four!

Chapter Eight
Does This Mean I'm Crazy?

"Let's go Annie," mom says, grabbing her keys from the side table and picking up her purse. She draped the purse over her left forearm and turned toward Annie.

Annie stared back.

Doctor. No Doctor!

"I feel fine, Mom." Annie countered.

Why the doctor today?

Maybe mom isn't feeling well.

That must be it; she does look a little gray.

Oh no!

"Mom, are you sick?" Annie asked somewhat panicked.

"No sweetie," mom hustled her toward the door, "we're going to be late."

"But why are we going if we aren't sick?" Annie queried.

"Honey, this isn't our usual doctor. We are going to go to a doctor that works with people's thoughts, feeling, and behaviors." Her mom said stopping and placing a hand on Annie's shoulder.

Her purse slipped forward and bonked Annie in the side of the head.

A head doctor!

A shrink?

Why does mom want to go to a head shrinker?

Annie had heard of head doctors. She'd run across Psychiatrist in the dictionary on one of her many groundings. She'd seen TV programs with Psychiatrist, but those people were crazy.

Weren't they?

Am I crazy?

Annie had always known she was different. Didn't she always feel left out or on the outside looking in?

Weren't friendships and social interactions difficult for her?

Maybe that was it!

Maybe I AM crazy!

Annie sees herself sitting on the floor in a room with no windows.

She is wearing a white coat-like thing with the sleeves too long. There are straps attached that tie behind her back forcing her to hug herself.

"We are going to talk with Dr. Caton about school," Annie's mom broke into her thoughts.

"Do you remember the conversation I had with Mrs. Jones a few months ago?" Mom asked.

Mm-hmm, Annie nodded.

"And you know that you've been bringing daily notes home," mom continued.

"Mm-hmm," another nod.

"And you remember when Mrs. Timpkins and Mrs. Meyer worked with you a few weeks ago?" Mom stopped and turned to Annie.

Annie had been pulled out of class a few times over the last couple of weeks. Mrs. Timpkins worked with Annie first. Mrs. Timpkins doesn't usually work at the school.

Annie had seen her around before. She has an office at the school with her name on the door and 'School Psychologist' under her name. Lately, she had been sitting in Annie's classroom on occasion. She never stayed very long though, maybe a half hour or so.

Annie wasn't sure what a school psychologist was, but thought that Mrs. Timpkins seemed like a very nice lady.

Mrs. Timpkins wore a suit and high heels. Most teachers wore more casual clothes, even jeans. Mrs. Timpkins carried a fancy looking briefcase and lots and lots of folders.

The first time Mrs. Timpkins came for Annie. She smiled nicely. She has a pretty smile with very shiny white teeth! Annie liked her smile.

Mrs. Jones acted strange that first day. She kept shaking Mrs. Timpkins' hand and saying, "Thank you. Thank you."

Annie wondered what Mrs. Jones might be thanking her for.

Mrs. Jones smiled very broadly at Annie and said, "This is Mrs. Timpkins. She is a very nice lady. She is going to be working with you for awhile."

Mrs. Jones frown lines seemed to smooth visibly.

Weird.

Annie turned to Mrs. Timpkins expectantly.

"Well Annie," Mrs. Timpkins put her hand gently on Annie's back nudging her in the other direction, "We are going to be spending some time together over the next couple of weeks. Is that okay?"

"Will I miss recess?" Annie asked.

"Not if we can help it." Mrs. Timpkins smiled.

"Will I miss music?" Annie asked.

"Not if we can help it." Mrs. Timpkins replied still smiling.

"PE?"

"Not if we can help it."

"Art?"

"Not if we can help it."

"Lunch?"

"Not if we can help it."

"Math?"

"Not if we can help it." Mrs. Timpkins wasn't smiling quite as brightly.

"Handwriting?

No response.

"Not science, I can't miss science. I even read my assignment. We are learning about photosynthesis.

I like learning about photosynthesis.

Do you know what photosynthesis is? See, plants use *conversion* to change unusable energy into…"

Mrs. Timpkins wasn't smiling, "Annie, how about we not worry so much about that right now?"

"But how do I know what to worry about if I don't know what to worry about?" Annie's circular logic seemed to take Mrs. Timpkins by surprise, because her eyebrows shot up in response.

Cool.

Mrs. Timpkins' eyebrows sort of disappeared into her hairline.

I wonder if my eyebrows disappear into my hair, Annie thought to herself raising her eyebrows up and down. When she raised them up, she felt around with her fingertips trying to gauge whether or not they would be visible or hidden.

Where is a mirror when you need one?

"Annie?"

"Hmm?" Annie replied automatically, still engrossed with her eyebrows.

"Annie," Mrs. Timpkins placed her hand on Annie's shoulder, "This is my office."

What? Oh yes, Annie knew this was the office.

"Would you care to step in and we can begin?" Mrs. Timpkins opened the door for Annie.

Inside was a wall full of cupboards and shelves. To the left was a long desk looking thing but it was attached to the wall. The desk thing circled around and sort of became a desk on the other side too.

Cool.

A comfy looking office chair sat encircled by the contraption. Dad would love that chair. He says if he doesn't get a better chair soon, he's going to be walking like an old man.

Dad's silly sometimes.

A big computer dominated most of the side desk area.

I wonder if it has neat games on it. Our computer has neat games, but last time I played on it there was a little problem. I thought if I pushed enough buttons, it would be fine. Dad turned the same weird color as Mrs. Jones does sometimes. He said I wasn't to be left alone with it EVER AGAIN… Someone clearing her throat interrupted Annie's thoughts.

Chapter Nine

Let the Testing Begin!

"Annie, would you care to have a seat?" Mrs. Timpkins was sitting at her desk in that big comfy chair.

How did she get there so fast?

Books were everywhere!

There were books on the desk, books on the shelves, books piled on the floor, there were even books covering the little round table over in the corner under the window.

Wow.

I like books. Books are my friends.

Mom says she won't buy me any more books, because it's going to put them in the poorhouse; so now we go to the library.

"Annie," Mrs. Timpkins was still waiting.

"Oh sorry?" Annie answers automatically.

Annie is very used to answering without knowing what the question was. She is getting good, she thinks, at context cues and trying to guess the appropriate response.

"Okay Annie, let's begin."

First Mrs. Timpkins asked Annie questions, like:

"What is your name?"

"What is your address?"

"What is your favorite color?"

"Do you have any brothers or sisters?"

She continued asking questions like this for about a half hour or so. Annie was feeling very itchy inside.

It is very hard to sit still for so long.

Annie continued to answer, but began to stare at the diplomas and certificates hanging on the wall above the side-desk with the computer.

Wow, that's a lot of certificates.

I wonder how many years Mrs. Timpkins was in school.

Did she like school?

She must have liked school, otherwise why would she have stayed so long? She must be in like 21st grade or something. I don't want to stay in school that long. I wonder if…

"Annie," Mrs. Timpkins was staring oddly at Annie.

"Annie what were you thinking of just then?"

Embarrassed, Annie didn't want to say.

How many times has she tried to explain to someone, that what she was thinking just now, was too broad of a question?

How do you explain that "just now" she may have thought about school, shopping, the Tylenol mom gave her with the numbers on them, and how did they get the numbers on them, and why did they put the numbers on them, and of the Romans and what they did if they had a headache because clearly THEY didn't have Tylenol, and if they had buckles on their shoes and if they called them shoes, and…

"Annie, can you tell me what you were thinking?" Mrs. Timpkins asked again.

"Um, can I go to the restroom?" Annie asked.

That one always works.

"Yes you may in just a bit. But first, Annie, I want you to tell me what was going through your mind," Mrs. Timpkins persisted.

Nervously, Annie began chewing on her right upper lip.

"Um, I was just thinking about all of your diplomas," Annie said lowering her eyes.

"What else, Annie?" Mrs. Timpkins prompted.

"Um, and Tylenol," Annie said still staring downward.

"Do you have a headache?" Mrs. Timpkins asked.

"No," Annie replied, "And Romans, and their shoes, and some other stuff too."

Mrs. Timpkins smiles and writes something down.

"Does your brain sometimes feel like it is going too fast?" Mrs. Timpkins asked, setting her pen down, and leaning towards Annie.

"Mm-hm," Annie nodded miserably.

"Like you have a thought and it leaps to another and another and you sometimes forget what is going on around you?" Mrs. Timpkins gently asked.

Exactly, how does she know?

The next few times they met, Mrs. Timpkins began with, "Today we are going to do a series of activities, and they start out very easy, and may become more difficult. It is okay to say, 'I don't know,' but I want you to give each and every activity your best effort."

Annie did some activities with blocks, shapes, mazes, codes, and answered lots of questions with Mrs. Timpkins.

Mrs. Timpkins sometimes used a stopwatch and other times there didn't seem to be any time limits.

Annie liked working with Mrs. Timpkins.

Annie wasn't quite as excited to work with Mrs. Meyer.

Mrs. Meyer had her do tests.

She did lots and lots of tests.

Annie did math tests, reading tests, writing tests, and listening tests. Mrs. Meyer didn't smile like Mrs. Timpkins.

Mrs. Meyer didn't say, "Good job "or" I like the way you are trying," or even "Thank you for your effort," like Mrs. Timpkins.

Mrs. Meyer said things like, "Why can't you just stay in your seat," and "Must you shake your foot like that," and "Honestly, you are giving me a headache could you not talk so much," and "Annie if you would just apply yourself..."

Annie had always felt bad about the, "Why can't you just's..."

"Why can't I just be normal? Why can't I just pay attention? Why can't I just find friends? Why can't I just fit in? Why can't I..." Mrs. Meyer interrupted Annie's thoughts.

"Annie, why can't you just finish so we can go back to your room? I have other kids coming in about ten minutes."

Sighing, Annie resolved herself to try harder.

Annie always felt like she was trying harder, but it never seemed to be good enough.

What was wrong with her?

"Why can't I just…"

Annie stared silently out of the window on the ride to Dr. Caton's office. Mom attempted conversation a couple of times, "So, how was your day?

Did you do anything special today?

What was for lunch?

Did you play with anyone at recess?"

Mom gave up after the series of monosyllabic replies by Annie.

What would the head-shrinker doctor do to Annie? Would he lock her up? Would he use needles? Annie shuddered involuntarily.

"Are you cold sweetie?" Mom asked, automatically adjusting the temperature dials.

I wonder if they had head-shrinkers back in the olden days. I know I read about the peddlers who sold 'snake oil' cures for people.

Annie is standing in the middle of a crowded, dusty street. Her long, flowery dress is muddied at the bottom from where she and Dougie crossed a puddle.

Dougie laughed and said he'd have thrown his cape across it for her safe passage, like the chivalrous knights, but he didn't own a cape!

Annie made a face at him and giggled.

Even if Dougie had a cape, it would probably be so worn and filled with holes, that it wouldn't have protected her one bit!

"Step right up!

Step right up!" The shouts, of the funny little man, hushed the crowd somewhat.

He was a slight man with dark, oily-looking hair. He had a fancy mustache, waxed to make it stand out straight from either side of his mouth.

He reminded Annie of a deranged catfish in a wig!

The greasy, little man was wearing impossibly white pants with knee boots, and a vest with red and white vertical stripes.

He had on a large top hat.

Behind him stood his wagon, colorfully painted, and overloaded with bottles of every size, shape, and color.

"Step right up!

Get a closer look!

Instant health, vitality, and youth!

Chapter Ten
Victoria Lilianne

"Right here!

Right here!"

The crowd shuffled a bit.

Muffled shouts of, "Snake oil!"

"Bah!"

"Drive on!"

Equally interspersed, were cries of, "How much?"

"Will it cure my gout?"

"Quiet down and let the man speak!"

Annie looked suspiciously at Dougie, "Cure all?

Do you think anything…"

"Annie."

Annie looked around.

The doctor's office!

Oh no.

"Okay Annie, we're here," mom said, grabbing her purse with one hand, while turning off the ignition and removing her keys with the other.

She sat back when she saw Annie's face, "It'll be okay. No needles today. I promise. We are just here to talk."

"What are we talking about?" Annie asked, with her face pressed tightly against the glass of her window, as she tried to see the doctor's office better.

"Well, sweetie," mom said kindly,

"we are going to talk about school, friends, and time."

"Time?" Annie turned and looked at her mom.

"Let's go," was the only response, as mom had already turned, and was opening the car door.

Annie's heart sank. She felt both hot and cold at once. Her heartbeat was a strong thump, felt throughout her entire body. Annie felt the familiar nausea and hollowness.

"Mom, I don't want to! I can't," Annie pleaded.

The familiar terror, at new situations and change, flooded through Annie. Her feet felt heavy and her chest tight.

Any kind of change unsettles Annie a LOT!

Once, Annie had come home from school to find that mom had rearranged the furniture. The couch was in a totally different spot and the rest of the chairs and tables were shuffled about.

"You BROKE it! Put it back!" Annie's exclamation came without thought or pretense. She was overwhelmed at the subtle difference in her environment.

Other little changes can equally rock her world. Even a change in schedule at school or an early dismissal can completely leave Annie discombobulated!

When she was little, and changed

from grade to grade, Annie would often find herself standing at the classroom of the previous grade, for the first few weeks of school. Her teacher from the previous year would smile questioningly and Annie would embarrassedly excuse herself and skulk back to the classroom at which she belonged.

Her mom took her hand and kept walking.

"No please mom, I'll be good. I'll try harder," Annie was flooded with panic.

They stopped at the front desk. Her mom asked for directions to Dr. Caton's office.

Annie looked around for the first time.

It was a beautiful building.

The ceilings were forever high and the windows sparkled as if newly cleaned. The receptionist beamed brightly at mom and gave instructions on how to find the appropriate suite.

They walked to the elevator in the middle of the floor. As they entered, Annie glanced back at the receptionist.

She was still smiling.

Nice lady.

Dr. Caton's suite was richly colored with dark wood paneling and furniture. The seat covers were burgundy with gold fleur-de-lis pattern. The drapes, carpets, and even prints on the walls had similar colors.

Annie thought it felt safe.

Interesting.

Annie had a seat in one of the deep comfortable chairs. There were magazines, books, puzzles, and even games. Annie had never been to a doctor's office that had so many things for kids.

Mom talked with the receptionist and then sat next to Annie.

They waited together in silence.

It was so quiet. No crying babies or coughing.

In a few short minutes, Annie heard her name called, "Victoria Lilianne?"

At first she didn't realize they were calling for her.

No one called her by her full name. At least no one called her by her full name, unless she was in trouble. When mom full named, middle named, or 'young-lady-ed' her, she KNEW she was in trouble.

They followed the pretty nurse back to an office. The room looked nothing like any doctor's office she'd ever seen. The carpet was just as thick and the chairs just as fancy as the waiting room. There was no examining table, x-ray-light thing, or clinical feel. There were no jars with cotton, swabs, or tongue depressors.

Annie and her mother sat in two of the big comfortable chairs. Annie's feet swung back and forth and her mom sat with her hands clutched tightly around the handles of her purse.

It was an old purse, one that Annie could remember back to when she was little. It was brown and made of soft leather. The handle was long and the purse rested at mom's hip when she stood or walked.

When Annie was little she'd developed the habit of using the purse as an armrest while holding on to the front part of the strap.

When Annie was little, she and her parents had visited South Dakota and Mount Rushmore. They also visited Snake Gardens.

Distracted, and a little frightened by the reptiles, Annie had meandered off from her parents. She had been watching and staring so intently, she didn't realize that mom and dad had gone on until she looked around to ask a question.

Finding herself alone in the steamy

enclosure, surrounded by snakes and other reptiles, Annie began to cry.

It was only for a moment or two, as mom and dad immediately missed her and rushed back, but it was enough. Annie was aware of her wandering attention and NEVER wanted to feel that lost again!

The purse/hand rest became the solution and worked well!

Annie's mind and eyes could wander, and her body stayed with mom!

Except for once at the state fair!

Annie walked with mom, admiring all around her. She looked from the balloons and hotdog venders, to the wild, high rides, and the laughing people.

Annie is an avid people-watcher.

Annie had let go of her mom's purse, for an instant, to get a better view of the man making funnel cakes. The thin stream of batter being swirled into the hot oil mesmerized her. Annie smiled as he lifted the cakes out with a new form and texture.

Awesome.

Annie reached back, without looking, to find the familiar armrest and continued walking.

Mom was not walking.

Annie stopped as well and looked questioningly up at mom.

Maybe mom wanted a funnel cake.

That is NOT mom! Annie panicked.

Annie's arm and hand rested on a STRANGER'S purse!

Mom and the strange woman smiled quizzically at each other and then down at Annie.

"Annie!"

"Oh sorry?" Annie's usual response to hearing her name called when she was 'in her own world.'

She had taken to calling it that, 'in her own world.' She liked it there. No one made fun of her. She did well in school there. She could…

"Annie," mom said, "this is Dr. Caton."

"Hello." The doctor said to Annie, reaching for her hand.

Why does she want my hand?

Oh, she wants to shake it.

Annie reached out as well saying,

"Nice to meet you."

Mom would be pleased with my impeccable manners, Annie thought as she shook the cool, firm hand of Dr. Caton.

Impeccable is a neat word. Annie liked the way it felt when she said "Im-PECC-able," with extra emphasis on the middle syllable.

"Pecc, pecc, pecc," Annie was mouthing the word.

"I'm glad to finally meet you Annie," Dr. Caton interrupted her thoughts, "Your mom and I have been talking about you."

You have?

Annie looked questioningly at mom.

"We have talked. And your mom has also been talking with the school," Dr. Caton was looking intently at Annie.

"Why do you think we've been talking and your mom has been meeting with your teachers?"

Annie's eyes dropped to her lap. She began chewing at her lip.

"Annie?"

"Because," Annie said softly, "I'm weird."

"What do you mean by 'weird,'" Dr. Caton asked as mom reached over and took Annie's hand, squeezing reassuringly.

Annie glanced up at mom, and then said, "I don't fit in. My teachers always get frustrated and mom gets notes."

"Do you have friends Annie," Dr. Caton asked in the same kind tone.

"Not really," Annie felt a sob rising in her chest, "I want to play and have friends. But, I always seem to mess things up."

The sob escaped. Mom squeezed her hand a little tighter.

"Tell me how you mess things up?"

"Well, sometimes I say things.

Other kids don't seem to like talking about the things I like. They say I'm 'interrupting.' I try to be quiet and listen, but my mouth blurts sometimes even when my brain is trying to be quiet," Annie mumbled almost inaudibly.

"You are a very intuitive person Annie," Dr. Caton said, "Do you know what intuitive means?"

"Good at sensing things or knowing what other people are thinking?" Annie ventured.

"Annie," Dr. Caton said shifting slightly in her chair, she leaned forward, "Are you smart?"

Annie shook her head vehemently, 'NO,' without verbalizing her shame.

Mom reached into her purse for a tissue.

"Annie, you are very, very smart," Dr. Caton smiled, "Do you know how I know?"

Annie looked at her wondering whom she must be talking about, because certainly she must be mistaken.

"Because I have test scores that PROVE you are smart, Annie. I know you don't believe me, especially since we just met. But your mom and the school decided that you might need some help. They did a battery of tests to see what might be going on," Dr. Caton asked, "Do you know what a battery of tests means?"

Annie scrunched the corner of her mouth and her left eyebrow,

"A bunch of different ones?"

Mom and Dr. Caton smiled at each other.

"Yes, a bunch of different ones. One of those tests measures *ability,*" she emphasized ability, "That means they compared the way you performed compared to other kids. The score compares you to lots of other kids. The scores are a way to measure the way you are expected to perform in school, compared to your peers."

Annie looked suspicious.

Chapter Eleven
Train Your Busy Brain

"Your mom also filled out some forms for us. They asked about lots of things like, 'Do you have difficulty sitting still and do you have trouble making decisions?'"

Annie looked at mom.

"The tests showed that you are very intelligent. You have an ability score that is way above average. That means that you should be performing better than most, if not all, of the kids in your classroom," Dr. Caton said.

Annie looked crestfallen, next would come the 'A' word.

"Why can't you just APPLY yourself Annie? Why can't you just TRY harder? Why can't you just…"

Dr. Caton interrupted Annie's thoughts, "The tests also showed us that you have some difficulty demonstrating how smart you really are. You struggle to pay attention and to organize your things. Do you lose things frequently, Annie?"

Annie and mom both laughed at that.

How many times had she heard, "Annie you would lose your head if it wasn't attached to your shoulders"?

Dr. Caton continued, "Your mom and I discussed the results and she asked if I would explain them to you. Annie, have you ever heard of something called Attention Deficit Disorder?"

Annie shook her head.

"Attention Deficit Disorder is a brain condition that causes you to forget things. It causes you to blurt and be impulsive. ADD, which is short for Attention Deficit Disorder, can make you feel weird inside of your own skin.

Sometimes people with ADD lack organizational skills and they have problems with social skills. Do you know what I mean when I say 'Social Skills'?"

Annie replied, "Please and thank you's?"

"Yes. Some of the social skills I am talking about include manners, but there are a lot more.

Sometimes, people with ADD need special help in learning and using social skills that seem to be so easy for everyone else."

"Annie, you have Attention Deficit Disorder. It is clear from all of the tests, observations, and parent reports that the diagnosis fits you," Dr. Caton said, looking directly into Annie's eyes.

"Does that mean I really am crazy," Annie asked, picturing a straight jacket again.

"No sweetie," mom immediately interjected.

"No. It doesn't mean that you are crazy at all. It means that your brain is very busy compared to other people.

It means that you may be more creative, think outside of the box more, and look at things and people, in a different way.

It means that your brain is kind of like a filing cabinet. Only the filing cabinet is too full and you have too many ideas and thoughts to store them all properly.

When you need to retrieve one of those thoughts or ideas from your 'filing cabinet' it is hard to find again."

Annie mulled the information over.

She wasn't crazy, but she was different.

Annie didn't WANT to be different.

She wants to fit in!

Annie doesn't want Mrs. Jones to get those frown lines when she looks at her or talks with her.

Annie wants to please her teachers and her parents.

She tries so hard.

Why can't she just be NORMAL?

"We can work together, if you would like, to learn some of those social skills. We can help to 'retrain your busy brain' to make good decisions and to keep track of stuff," Dr. Caton offered brightly, "Would you like to work with me on some of those things?"

Annie nodded, with tears hovering in her eyes, "Will it help me make friends?"

"Yes, Annie, I believe it will. We will work together on steps to help you socially.

We will learn how to accept 'no' for an answer. We will learn how to enter a conversation or group appropriately.

We will learn lots of techniques to help you be more successful in school, at home, and with friends.

We will help you with organizational strategies, so you really can show how very smart you are!"

How can she be so sure?

"I have ADD too, Annie," Annie jumped, and looked up, as Dr. Caton shared this.

"I was diagnosed later in life. I never got the help I needed when I was your age. People didn't understand the disorder back then.

I didn't understand either. I struggled for most of my life, to try harder or apply myself, just like you."

Annie looked on, in wonderment.

"ADD can make you very sad if you don't understand;" Dr. Caton said gently, "You and your mom are very brave to be getting help."

Mom and Annie smiled at each other.

Looking at mom briefly, Dr. Caton turned back to Annie, "When you have a headache that won't go away, what does your mom give you?"

"An aspirin," Annie said.

"If you have an ear infection, what does the doctor prescribe?"

"Antibiotics," Annie said grimacing.

She HATES the taste of antibiotics!

"Well Annie, the pills you take to make you better, are necessary, right? They help to 'fix' the problem."

Annie nods.

"There is a pill to help 'train your busy brain' as well. The pills will help to slow your brain down, by speeding up."

What?!

That doesn't make sense.

"The medicine is called a 'stimulant.' The medication can help you slow down and think, before you act or say things that might get you into trouble. They will help you to focus on a task and get things done.

The pills will help you to begin projects, that would normally overwhelm you, and make you confused as to how to get started."

Annie looked at mom.

Mom nodded at her with a smile.

I could be NORMAL?

"Annie, have you ever seen someone

in a wheel chair?"

A nod.

"Do you think that person would get up, out of that chair, and walk if they could?"

A more emphatic nod.

"Well Annie, that wheel chair is kind of like your ADD. No matter how hard that person tried, he still wouldn't be able to walk.

The same is true for us, no matter how hard we try; we can't walk out of our busy brains. But we can do things to help us behave and feel more normal," Dr. Caton said the magic word.

Normal?!

"Would you like to try taking a pill to help you feel better," Dr. Caton asked.

Oh YES!

"What would it feel like," Annie asked instead.

"I didn't start taking medication for ADD until I was much older. In fact, it wasn't until I was in my Doctoral program that I understood my own brain. I began taking a medication to help me feel and behave more *NORMAL*. At first, I really didn't like it at all."

Annie looked on intently.

Dr. Caton looked thoughtful as she began, "I felt a squeezing pressure on my brain. It felt like my brain was different, altered.

I didn't like it. But, after a few days, that sensation went away.

Have you ever been to an eye doctor?"

Annie was surprised at the apparent change of topic, "Yes."

"Do you remember how the eye doctor asked you to look through one lens first and then through another?"

Mom and Annie both nodded.

"Do remember how he would ask, 'Number one or number two?' and you were supposed to tell him which lens you could see better through?"

More nods of agreement.

"Do you remember how you may have thought you could see fine through number one, until you looked through number two?"

"Yes," Annie said, wondering where Dr. Caton was going with this.

"Well, the medication for ADD is kind of like that second lens. You think you can see fine through the first lens, until you see through that second lens. Only when you see better, do you know what it was like with the first.

Only after you take a medication that lets you feel and act differently, do you understand what your brain felt like before."

Annie thought carefully about all that the doctor was saying.

Chapter Twelve
Will I Be A Zombie?

"Will the medicine help for sure," she asked.

"Most people with ADD are helped by medication. In fact, nine out of ten people who take stimulants report improvement. But there are lots of different medications.

Sometimes we have to try different kinds, or doses, to find the best fit. Not every medication is right for every person. That is why we will have to meet at least once a month, and your mom will call to let me know how things are going, in between our visits," Dr. Caton said nodding at mom.

She continued, "You will need to talk with your mom about anything you feel. You will need to tell her if you feel sadder, or if you have difficulty eating. Sometimes people lose weight when they start on a stimulant medication, so we will have to monitor that closely."

Mom nodded and looked at Annie, "We will keep a close eye on her weight."

"Do you want to try taking the medicine," Dr. Caton asked and mom leaned in.

Both women were looking intently at Annie.

What if it doesn't work?

Will it take away all of my thoughts?

What if I'm too different?

Can it really be that helpful?

What does it taste like?

"Does it taste bad," she asked aloud.

"Most come in a pill form. If you can swallow a pill, it doesn't taste at all. Some people experience dry mouth or a 'tin taste' for the first several weeks, but that usually subsides," Dr. Caton answered.

"Would everybody have to know?" She worried that she would be made fun of if the kids thought she was taking pills for her brain.

"No. The pills now come in an extended release form, meaning you can take one pill in the morning, and it will last through the school day.

You won't have to go to the office to take a pill during the school day, so no one but you and your family has to know," Dr. Caton reassured her.

Annie asked, "Will I feel like a zombie?"

She pictured herself wandering the hallways with a blank stare.

"At first you will feel the pressure of your brain that we talked about. The first day or two that you are left alone with your own brain, with the actual ability to concentrate and think clearly, will feel strange.

It may be a little frightening to feel what other people feel. As bright as you are, it may be a little scary for you," Dr. Caton replied, "That feeling and those fears will pass. If you don't feel better after a few weeks, we will discuss different options."

Mom finally spoke, "Will she need to take it every day?"

Turning to mom, Dr. Caton said, "She doesn't have to take if everyday, but I do recommend it. It will help her, emotionally, to maintain the chemical titration at a consistent level."

Looking at Annie she explained, "Chemical titration means the amount of the medication in your bloodstream."

Turning again to mom, "Rebound effect can occur. Rebound is what happens when her brain is sort of sling- shotting around, as the dose is leaving her system. Her serotonin level, nor epinephrine, and/or dopamine levels, her body's natural antidepressants, can be impacted.

So she may appear to be more depressed or cranky, as the medication is leaving her system. Sometimes, regular physical activity or exercise program can help to regulate this somewhat.

I've personally found that walking on the treadmill during that part of the day has eliminated the problem for me. If I can't walk on the treadmill or get physical exercise for some reason, a handful of peanut M&M's do the trick! Everyone is different, so we will have to monitor her closely."

Silence for a few moments.

"Do you have any other questions for me," she asked, looking back and forth between Annie and her mother.

Annie turned, and she and her mother raised their eyebrows at each other. Both then shook their heads 'no,' first to each other, then to Dr. Caton.

"You have asked some very important and thoughtful questions. As I said earlier, it is very clear that you are extremely bright and intuitive. I am glad that you are thinking very seriously about this decision.

Why don't I write a prescription for you? You and your family can discuss the decision further. If you choose to try the medication, your mom will already have the script. If you choose not to try, just shred the prescription. Please let me know either way."

Annie and her mom nodded.

"I would like to schedule to meet with you weekly, for a while, to work on social skills and organizational strategies. We will monitor her progress and will be able to meet less frequently as she learns the coping skills and shows improvement at school and with friendships."

Dr. Caton stood. She reached out a hand to mom, and shaking hands, they smiled at each other.

"Thank you so much for meeting with us," mom said to Dr. Caton.

"It was my pleasure to meet with both of you," she looked down at Annie, "I am especially pleased to have met you, Annie.

I think that you will be a much happier girl when we can train your busy brain and help you to feel more successful with school and friends."

Annie beamed up at her.

Could it be possible?

Could she really feel normal?

Mom placed her hand at the small of Annie's back, scooting her towards the door.

"Please make an appointment with my secretary for next week. We will begin with the social skill 'How to enter a conversation,'" Dr. Caton said.

Mom and Annie passed through the narrow hallway towards the secretary's desk. The carpet felt very thick and comforting underneath Annie's feet.

Stopping at the front desk, Mom made arrangements for Annie to come back after school the following week to begin her sessions with Dr. Caton.

As they left the office and walked through the building, Annie reached for Mom's hand. She squeezed it, while lost in thought.

What if the kids at school found out?

Would they laugh at her?

Would they think she was stupid or crazy?

What if it did help?

What if she could get better and make friends?

What if her teachers smiled at her and said she was a good student instead of the awful notes about applying herself, and the 'Why can't she just's'?

Annie felt mom squeezing her hand, breaking into her thought process.

"What do you think honey," she asked looking intently into Annie's eyes.

"I think that I hope what she said is true. I think that I hope I can be like everybody else," Annie replied.

"Oh Annie, I would never want you to be like everyone else. I like that you are my unique and interesting little girl. I am happy that your brain is the way it is. I would never want you to be any other way!

But, if the medicine and social skills training can help you to feel happier and make you feel like you fit in, then I am very excited to give it a try," mom laughingly hugged Annie close.

Annie looked up at her mom, "Me too!"

Chapter Thirteen
What Now?

"Annie?"

"Yes, Mrs. Jones?" Annie responded without looking up from the paper she was finishing.

She remembered her name at the top, and was very pleased with herself.

She had been pleased with herself for a while now. She had been getting papers turned in on time, even the ones that took days or weeks to complete. The enormity of any big projects wasn't overwhelming her.

In the past, Annie would be so overwhelmed by a large or lengthy project that she couldn't ever seem to begin.

Now, she just dove in and that was that!

The furrows between Mrs. Jones' eyebrows didn't appear nearly as often. Mrs. Jones' seldom had the hands on hips, glaring posture when she talked with Annie now.

The notes home were no longer needed, and the horrible pit in her stomach 'fear' Annie had so often had on the ride home was no longer present.

At first, Annie had really NOT liked the pills and how they made her feel.

Annie began taking them on a weekend. Dr. Caton recommended a weekend so mom could monitor and watch for side effects.

When Annie woke up, mom handed her a small blue and white capsule and a glass of water.   Annie swallowed the pill and waited.

Nothing.

What if it doesn't work?

What if it does work?

What…

"Annie, let's go have breakfast," mom had interjected.

Annie felt nothing for an hour or so, but then she felt…different.

She felt fuzzy, not quite right, but not quite wrong either.

Annie had a difficult time answering questions her mom asked as they walked through the grocery store that morning.

She felt…entranced. She felt entranced by her own brain. She felt like there was a pressure on her brain, but also that she could really THINK.

She was able to think about SOMETHING, not eight million something's at once. It made her feel kind of irritated when anyone intruded on her entrancement.

It was hard to give up that feeling to the intrusion of questions by others.

The feeling lasted most of the morning. She tried at first to "see through it." It was kind of like she had glasses on that were too strong for her.   She mentally tried to fight the effects of her medication at first.

She knew what to expect after Dr. Caton explained it to her, but it was still very disconcerting for the first few weeks.

Annie also noticed that when peopled talked to her; she didn't feel quite as anxious inside.

Normally, when people talked to her she felt uncomfortable. She felt like putting her hand over her mouth constantly, and she giggled too much.

Even when nothing funny was said, she giggled nervously. Annie normally felt awkward around anyone who wasn't family. She felt pressured about what she might say wrong, or forget to say, or say too loudly.

After most, if not all conversations, Annie mentally kicked herself for things she said or didn't say.

Why didn't I ask more about them?

Why did I say that?

Why didn't I say…?

It was easier to avoid talking with people and social settings, than to experience the way she beat herself up afterwards.

Now, Annie noticed that she didn't feel the need to cover her face when she talked with people. She could ask questions and fit into the conversation better. Annie didn't get upset with herself about everything she said or didn't say.

"This is a very good thing," Annie murmurs to herself.

Annie did have a difficult time eating normally for the first few weeks.

She sort of hovered between being ravenous at odd times, usually around 10:00 in the morning; other times she was borderline nauseous.

Annie learned to snack lightly throughout the day. At night, after the medication had worn off, she was able to eat a normal supper with her family. Dr. Caton said that she was pleased when they met. Annie had lost a little weight, but appeared to be maintaining well. Dr. Caton said that if she lost too much weight they would have to discontinue the medication.

Annie found that she could write more easily. She could sit down and actually finish a paper instead of jumping up to get something, wandering, daydreaming, or thinking of thirty new topics. Mrs. Jones appeared to be very pleased with this in particular.

"Annie, I am very proud of the effort you clearly put into your report on the Aztecs," Mrs. Jones had said in front of the whole class just last week!

Annie had been very pleased, and her cheeks turned pink at the praise.

Sometimes Annie missed her old self though.

Sometimes she missed being able to be lost in her own thoughts and the creativity she felt. Annie missed her "own world" sometimes. Annie couldn't flit from one topic to another as easily.

"Annie," Mrs. Jones touched Annie's shoulder lightly.

Somewhat startled, Annie replied,

"Yes, Mrs. Jones?"

"Would you like to go with Miss Timpkins now?" Mrs. Jones was still smiling down at her.

It was so nice to see Mrs. Jones smiling, instead of her usual pucker-faced, frown-line expression.

Mrs. Jones smiled at Annie a lot more now. She called on Annie more readily, as she no longer needed to scold Annie to wait her turn, at least not as often.

Annie didn't feel as embarrassed when she answered questions in front of her peers. She didn't feel the same compunction to blurt answers or give lengthy litanies.

"Where are we going?" Annie asked.

"Oh, well, I'm not exactly sure," Mrs. Jones said, "But I'm sure Miss Timpkins will be able to explain."

Annie walked out of the classroom and down the hallway. It was a large hallway with high ceilings. Annie had walked down the same hallway since she was in Kindergarten.

In the past, entering the school building and walking down the hallways had given Annie a yucky feeling in the pit of her stomach.

The other students bustling by had unnerved her somewhat. The jostling and locker banging left Annie feeling disoriented and edgy.

Annie had never noticed that any of the other students looked to be affected by the experience. In fact, Annie had often marveled at how they milled along, seemingly oblivious to the turmoil Annie had boiling throughout.

It their defense, Annie had perfected the art of pasting on a half-amused smile. She had adopted the affective façade early on in life. It was easier to assume the expression of complacence, than to constantly try and explain herself.

"What's wrong Annie?"

"Why are you scared?"

"Does your stomach hurt?"

"Was someone mean to you?"

Annie had tried and failed to describe her feelings over the years. How do you tell a teacher that, yes she had forced the other children to include Annie, but when Annie went to play with them, she didn't have a clue HOW to play together!

When Annie was in Kindergarten, and was trying to join a group of kids, they had told her, "No, you can't play with us. We only play with our friends."

Annie had tried to protest that she was their friend too. She became more and more upset, as she was seemingly incapable of making her point understood to the others.

When the recess aide intervened, Annie told her that they were being hypocrites because some were allowed into their little group and others were excluded without cause.

The recess aide made Annie stand by the wall for the rest of the recess for using words that she didn't understand.

Annie was crushed.

In first grade Annie had complained

to her teacher that the other girls weren't letting her play with them on the swings. When Miss Krentz, their teacher, instructed the others to include Annie, they had grumbled.

For a few minutes, Annie swung on the swings next to them. Then, unceremoniously, they left as a group. Annie tried to act like she didn't care, but the tears hovering in her eyes gave her away.

"Why can't I just be normal?"

"Why can't I just fit in?"

"Why can't I…."

Annie couldn't remember a time in her life that the familiar chant hadn't been a part of her existence.

By the time Annie was in second

grade, she had her own little box. Not a
figurative box, but a real one. It was an old
stove box. They placed it over Annie in her
desk and cut out a 'window' in the front to
allow Annie to see the teacher.

A study carrel they had called it.

"Annie can't seem to keep from
talking to her neighbors."

"Annie's fidgeting is distracting to the
other students."

"Annie needs extra barriers to help
her focus when I am teaching."

A list of reasons for the entrapment
was provided. What wasn't provided was
the cushion for the blow to Annie's self-
esteem. Also not provided was the
protection from the taunts of other students.

"What's the matter box girl?"

"Did they let you out of your cage?"

"Hey weirdo, what's it like in there?"

Annie suffered the jabs with a smile, pretending that she thought they were funny. Annie never thought they were funny. She knew she was different, and the box simply proved it to her and everyone else.

Chapter Fourteen
A Time for Friends

Annie arrived at Miss Timpkins' office just before lunchtime. The door was closed. Annie wondered if she should wait, or if she should knock.

Staring indecisively and chewing on her lip, Annie stood paralyzed outside of the door.

Just as she decided to knock, the door opened.

Miss Timpkins stood inside holding the door open in an inviting manner.

Annie smiled and walked in.

Sitting around the room in a semi-circle were several other students. Annie recognized a few of them.

John was at the end of the row on the left. He was in the grade above Annie. She remembered that John was frequently in trouble when they were younger for eating Chap Stick!

Apparently, one of John's favorite foods was flavored Chap Stick. He would sneak into the closet at school and rifle through the girls' backpacks. Any flavored Chap Stick, gloss, or other lip accoutrement was then fair game for John to devour.

He wasn't even subtle about it!

John would emerge from the closet munching away without seeming to mind that others saw him! When the owner of the various lip products would exclaim in outrage, John would grin and smack his lips.

John was a frequent visitor to the principal's office.

Sitting next to John, was Terry. Terry was in John's grade as well. Terry was a very shy girl. She was very sick when she was in 2nd grade and Annie was in Kindergarten.

Terry had missed a lot of school that year and was held back. Terry had always seemed nice, but she didn't ever say a lot. She was kind of a loner, and Annie had never seen her playing with other kids.

Jason sat next to Terry. Jason was what the other kids called, an 'odd duck.' Jason liked to talk endlessly about topics that were only of interest to him.

He would get on a topic like World War II, the Titanic, or Egyptology and chatter on endlessly without expression or noticing that no one else seemed to listen.

Jason repeated phrases like, "Oopies" or "Aren't I funny?" He was also, apparently, overly concerned about smells. Jason sniffed his fingers repeatedly. He also liked to smell his food, his pencils, his pencil box, and pretty much anything and everything else that he came into contact with.

Samantha sat next to Jason. Samantha had just moved to the school a few months earlier. Her parents had just gotten divorced and she moved with her mom and sisters to the district. Samantha looked sad a lot. She always had large, dark circles under her eyes and she almost never smiled.

Annie recognized most of the other children, but didn't know them all by name. She looked up questioningly at Miss Timpkins.

"Please have a seat Annie," she said with her hand outstretched toward the group of students.

Annie was surprised to see that they all smiled in a welcoming manner. Samantha didn't smile with the rest, but she didn't look reluctant either.

"Okay everyone," Miss Timpkins said; taking a seat with everyone, "Almost everyone is here. Let's get started, I'm sure our other friend will join us soon."

The rest of the students shifted in their seats forming a tighter circle by bringing the chairs around.

One chair was left empty.

Annie assumed it must be for the missing student, referred to by Miss Timpkins.

"Let's talk again about why we are here. A few of you are brand new to our little group and are probably wondering why you are here," Miss Timpkins said brightly.

"We are here to talk about Friendship. Can anyone tell us more?" Miss Timpkins glanced around the room.

"Friendship…Friendship is a unique and high-level social relationship with a myriad of interpretations depending on the audience.

The perceptions of friendship will vary among individuals as a result of their different social experiences and expectations. Most friendships entail certain common attributes that distinguish friendship from acquaintances and other social relationships. A friendship manifests as an affective tie between two individuals. Friends may choose each other freely, and it is mutual, reciprocal, consistent, and enduring." Jason recited in a monotone, without changing expression or inflection.

"Good Jason," Miss Timpkins affirmed, "Friendship plays an important role for us throughout our lifetime. Friendships may let us share affection, support, companionship, and assistance."

The other students nodded.

"Can anyone else say a little about friendship?" Miss Timpkins again looked around the room.

Raising her hand, Terry said shyly, "By playing together and interacting, children teach each other social skills and make each other feel like they belong."

"Wonderful," Miss Timpkins smiled at Terry, "Anyone have anything to add?"

Jason nodded, "Friendship is often demonstrated behaviorally as noted by shared participation in leisure activities. Recreation and leisure activity appears to be a medium in which friendships develop and flourish."

"Very good Jason. We are a 'Circle of Friends.' We try to help each other to feel like we belong. We work together on social skills and fitting in. All of us here have some difficulty or feel like we are different in some way," Miss Timpkins said, smiling warmly around the room, "We work together to learn how to build relationships as we believe that relationships are very important in life. We are using our peers to problem solve and learn from each other. The most important part of our Circle of Friends is that everyone here is here by choice. We are all willing to work together to help each other."

Annie looked around the room, appearing to be confused.

Noticing the confusion on Annie's face, Miss Timpkins asked, "Annie, do you have a question for us?"

"I have never heard of this group. How did you all find each other, and how did this start?" And, why haven't I always been included, Annie finished the last part silently to herself.

"Well, some of us are here at the recommendation of a teacher. Others are here because a friend brought them. The rest are here because they heard about the group and hoped to join us," Miss Timpkins replied, "We decided to set up a circle of friends to create a support network that would become natural friendships."

The other students nodded emphatically.

"We discussed what we wanted to accomplish and what we hoped would happen. We began the Circle of Friends last September with five students. We have grown to the size of the group here, with the exception of one, who is still coming.

The reason we keep growing in size is that other students have heard about what we are doing. They want to be a part of our Circle of Friends. We won't deny anyone who wishes to participate and be a part of our group. We meet weekly to celebrate each other's successes, achievements, and difficulties.

We also meet to organize activities outside of school. Sometimes we plan a movie, skating, or other outing. This helps us to generalize what we've learned together. Does anyone want to explain what I mean by *generalizing?*" Miss Timpkins looked around.

Samantha glanced up, without smiling, "It means to take what we learn here and demonstrate it in other settings, like after school, in class, or at home."

"Very, *very* good, Samantha," Miss Timpkins beamed.

Chapter Fifteen
Social Acceptance…could it really be?

"When I started the school year, I didn't have the confidence to speak to anyone. I couldn't look anyone in the eye and I constantly felt nervous. I felt like I was invisible and vulnerable. I felt totally isolated and desperate," Samantha continued, as Terry and Annie nodded sympathetically, "Since being in the Circle of Friends, I feel more able to be outgoing.

I even sometimes sit with friends at lunch; I never would have done that before!

166

I never would have thought that I had friends to sit with!"

Annie had never heard Samantha say so much before!

"We learn Social Skills too," Miss Timpkins said, "Anyone want to talk about Social Skills?"

Annie spoke up, "I know this! Dr. Caton told me about Social Skills!"

She was immediately contrite and embarrassed that she blurted out.

However, no one seemed to be annoyed.

If anything, they looked pleased at her participation, even Miss Timpkins seemed to be looking on with encouragement, rather than censure.

"It means learning the skills to join friends, participate in social situations, engage adults and peers in conversation, and use body language in different environments," Annie rushed out hoping to be right.

"Excellent!" Miss Timpkins exclaimed, "Using these techniques and practicing together can help us feel more confident and others will genuinely enjoy being around us!"

Annie hoped to herself that all of this could be true for her!

Terry quietly raised her hand, "It may not seem like it, but our Circle of Friends has helped me to understand my own unique talents and attributes.

They have helped me to be more willing to take risks in class and more open to answering questions."

Oh please me too!

Miss Timpkins added, "Our little group has surprised many of the staff with our new enthusiasm for learning and the great strides we appear to have made together.

I have heard the comments, 'He/she wants to learn now.

He/she is showing inquisitiveness now, and it is very rewarding for me to observe this development and growth.'"

How exciting!

John spoke up, "My attendance at school is now excellent according to the principal.

I actually look forward to coming to school and I even miss my friends in the group during the holidays.

I NEVER thought I'd say THAT!"

Everyone laughed together.

It felt good.

Annie liked to be laughing with everyone, instead of being laughed at and then pretending it didn't bother her!

Miss Timpkins continued, "Terry is right. She has become much more outgoing. Last week her classroom teacher said to me, 'Terry has become a more confident young lady. She is beginning to express her opinion both inside and outside of class.'

Did you ever think you would hear that remark in regard to yourself?"

Everyone, not just Terry, shook their heads emphatically and laughed.

"One of the reasons that our little Circle of Friends has been so successful is because of the commitment and enthusiasm of everyone involved.

We all try to see beyond each other's difference, focus instead of the need to belong and supportive," Miss Timpkins said, "We are all proud of the progress that we have made together and individually.

It is a great feeling to have best friends and feel like a peer in school rather than an outcast.

Right?"

More nods around the room.

Jason intoned, again without inflection, "The Circle of Friends has been very important to me. We are able to share both good and bad things with each other. We can discuss issues and spend a lot of time together. It is fun to help new kids with their problems too."

Miss Timpkins positively beamed at Jason, "Wonderful! We are working together on something called Social Inclusion.

Social Inclusion means the ability to gain social acceptance and to be able to interact positively with our peers.

Enjoying activities with friends, making new friends, and the overall feeling of 'fitting in' is our highest goal together.

Another goal for our little Circle of Friends is to have a welcoming, accommodating group that is conducive to helping make friends and sharing experiences, in a non-threatening environment."

Oh happy day!

"Even though, individually, we all have some difficulty in seeking and maintaining friendships, as a group, I believe we can reach our goals, since we have similar needs and the desire to be successful," Miss Timpkins announced.

Samantha interjected quietly, "I have already seen how the Circle of Friends has helped me, both at school and at home.

Before, right after my mom left my dad, I felt alone, even at home. I felt like I couldn't talk to anyone, and that I didn't want to.

Now, I spend more time with my family and feel closer to them."

Everyone clapped suddenly.

Annie jumped.

Noticing the startled response, Miss Timpkins quickly reached across the circle, and patted Annie's knee, "That's what we do.

We celebrate our successes together. Sometimes we clap, sometimes we smile, and sometimes we even shout and jump around.

No one judges, and no one puts other down, in our Circle of Friends. These are some of our rules and we all take them very seriously."

No one judges?

Could it really be?

"We call it our 'fertile ground for friendship development.' We are even planning on planting a tree at the end of the school year, to symbolize the success of our group.

We are going to break down the barriers keeping us from friendships and happiness, and build up the frequency with which we make positive interactions," Jason finished his recitation without expression, but no one seemed to mind.

No one called him names.

No one laughed or snickered behind their hands.

Oh happy, HAPPY day!

"We hope that the friendships started and nurtured in this room, will spill out into the hallways, and even outside of school.

We hope to maintain the friendships into the summer, and even following grades," Miss Timpkins suddenly looked expectantly at Annie, "Would you like to join our Circle of Friends, Annie?"

Just as Annie started to answer, the door flew open behind her.

Annie jumped and turned in her seat.

Chapter Sixteen
A Friend for Annie

"Dougie!" The group called out, as Annie breathed the name simultaneously.

"Hi guys! Sorry I'm late!" Dougies' hair was sticking out in all directions and his broad grin filled his face,   "I   got caught up with the guys, they asked if I'd shoot some hoops with them."

The room immediately erupted in laughter and clapping.

"All right Dougie!"

"Cool man!"

"Nice!"

"You 'da man!"

Miss Timpkins shushed the group after a few minutes of merriment, "All right everyone, let's let Dougie continue," turning to Annie she asked, "Do you know Dougie?"

Do I know him?!

Of course I know him!

He is so nice and so cute!

Aloud she simply said, "Yes, he sits behind me."

Dougie grinned broadly at Annie, "Annie's my girl! She says the smartest stuff in class!

She always knows the answer!

I don't know why Mrs. Jones doesn't call on her more often or why she sends her out to the hall so much. Well at least she used to. You don't go to the hall so much anymore, do you Annie?"

Dumbfounded, Annie stared at Dougie.

My girl?

Says smart stuff?

What was he saying?

"Anyway, like I was saying, the guys asked me to shoot hoops! I even made a few! It was great, they asked if I'd play again, but I said only on days I'm not with you guys," Dougie reached over and slapped Jason and John on the knees.

Jason's hands flapped around a bit in response and John tried to look unaffected, but he was grinning slightly.

"Well it looks like it's about time to

head back to class," Miss Timpkins turned again to Annie. "Well, Annie, what do you think? Would you like to join our Circle of Friends?"

Everyone turned towards Annie.

Dougie, especially, seemed to look at Annie intently.

"Yes! I would love to be a part of the group! Thank you so much for asking me!" Annie exclaimed unabashedly.

The group members smiled.

Dougie beamed!

"Well then! That's all settled. Welcome to our Circle of Friends Annie! We are so happy to have you as a new friend," Miss Timpkins said, rising to her feet.

"Back to class with you all. We will see you, same time and same place, next week," she opened the door for them to exit.

Filing out, the group of friends laughed and joked easily together.

Annie felt so good to be a part of a group. She was used to being beside a group, behind a group, sometimes accidentally mixed up into a group; but she had never before felt like PART of a group.

Annie felt happy.

She had friends!

It was a good day.

Epilogue

"Mom!"

"Mo-om, I'm HOME!" Annie called out, as she flew through front door, the screen door slamming into the side of the house behind her.

Annie winced at the CRACK!

Oops, have to remember to hold onto that silly door in the wind, she grimaced to herself.

"Hey boy!" Annie laughed, as Jesse settled his oversized paws directly on her shoulders.

Still laughing, she cried out, "How's my big boy?"

Jesse responded by slathering Annie with a giant-sized dog kiss. Wiping at her slobber covered cheek, she giggled.

"I missed you too, boy!"

"Annie? Is that you, sweetie?" Mom called from somewhere in the house.

"Yeah mom, I'm home!" Annie fairly flew through the front room, into the kitchen, where her mom was standing at the counter.

Spotting her mother, Annie rushed at her, wrapping her arms around her mom's waist from behind.

Annie hugged her mom, rocking from side to side.

"Oh hey now," her mom laughed, and raised her hands away from Annie.

In the middle of making, what appeared to be homemade noodles, Annie's mom's hands were covered in flour.

Extricating herself, while simultaneously wiping her hands on a dishtowel, mom turned into Annie's hug more fully.

She wrapped her arms around Annie, kissing the top of her head.

"Good day, kiddo?"

"The absolute BEST mom! It was magnificent, marvelous, monumental, majestic, and utterly STUPENDOUS!" Annie cried, releasing her mother.

Spinning around, with her head tipped back, and her arms outstretched, Annie cried, "It was the best, simply the BEST day. I went to the Circle of Friends. They were nice to me mom. I mean really nice, not just nice like when Mrs. Jones says they have to include me and they pretend to for awhile, but I can tell they don't really want to-nice, the REAL nice. The 'they-really-want-to-because-they-really-DO-like me,' kind of nice!"

Mom smiled, but there were tears in her eyes.

Not noticing, Annie continued to spin, "And they meet weekly, mom. And they do stuff together. Real stuff, like hang out, eat together, they even go to movies and things, sometimes. Can you imagine, mom? Can you just imagine? I might actually have friends, mom. Real friends!"

A single, lone tear coursed down mom's cheek, although she quickly dashed it away, still smiling at her daughter.

The joy she felt inside was indescribable.

How long had she hoped for her child to feel happiness at school?

How long had she prayed that Annie would come home and feel proud of herself?

How long had she wanted her child to find real friendship and to understand what a beautiful, delightful, wonderful little creature she was?

"That's wonderful, I'm so happy you had a good day," mom said, hiding the quiver in her voice and her bursting chest.

"Oh I did, mom, I really did. And did I tell you that Dougie is in the group? You remember Dougie?

He's the one who is nice to me. He sits behind me. He has a big goofy grin, mom. He never makes fun or calls me names. He is the one I told you about. You remember, right mom?" Annie said, in a breathless rush.

Annie's mom sagged against the counter, as joy, relief, and love filled her, as she looked at her daughter. The anxiety and worry were gone for a change, as she realized that Annie truly had a good day.

There would be no nasty-gram from Mrs. Jones today. There would be no scolding for Annie and no punishment for some infraction committed at school.

It would be a good evening. They would be able to enjoy each other without the stress of negative, 'school-issues' weighing in.

"Why don't you go put your things away and get started on your homework?" Mom said, turning back to her noodle making.

"I already did it mom," Annie sang out brightly.

"What?!" Mom spun around, again with surprise registering across her face.

"Yeah! I got it done in class," Annie called out, as she took the stairs, two at a time, on the way up to her room.

Annie didn't see her mother sag against the counter again, a look of disbelief and pleasure on her face.

Finished it in school?

Imagine that!

Annie's mom began to hum to herself as she finished making dinner. Mom didn't remember the last time she felt so happy.

Our girl had a good day.

Imagine that!

Jesse tore up the stairs behind Annie. His big, overgrown body flinging her to the wall of the stairwell.

"Easy there big guy," Annie laughed out.

"You'll break my ribs if you keep that up!"

Jesse beat her up the stairs, and turned to watch her progress, with his big pink tongue lolling out.

Later, Annie heard her father's truck pull into the drive.

Sprinting down the stairs, with Jesse in hot pursuit, Annie raced through the house, and flung herself into his arms.

"Ooph, kiddo! You're getting a little big for that," her dad said jokingly, "I think you broke a couple of ribs that time!"

"Guess what, dad! Just guess, you'll never guess. I made friends today dad! Real honest to goodness friends!" Annie rushed on breathlessly, "And I might get to go out sometimes and see them and we will meet once a week for lunch, and sometimes we can sit together even when we aren't in the group and…."

"Whoa, whoa…your old, tired dad just stepped in the door! You are going to have to take a breath, slow down, and tell me again what you are going on about!"

Annie took a deep breath, as instructed, and blew it out noisily and exaggerated for her dad's benefit, and began again, "It's called the Circle of Friends, Dad. They meet once a week and sometimes more. They help each other learn social skills and I knew what that was because Dr. Caton explained it and I explained it to them and they weren't upset that I blurted, dad, and…"

"Whoa, sweetheart, you are speeding again," dad ruffled her hair affectionately.

Taking another deep breath, Annie continued, "They are really nice. They clapped for each other and they didn't judge each other even when Jason started flapping his hands around.

Dougie walked back to class with me after. He said he was glad I'd be in the group, dad. He said he was happy that he'd see me sometimes after school!"

"I'm not so sure I want my little girl dating," Dad exclaimed with mock horror, "What does this kid do for a living? Does he drive? How does he intend to provide for my little girl?"

"Daa-ad," Annie giggled and rolled her eyes.

"No I mean it! What are his intentions? Do I need to have a talk with this boy?" Dad continued to tease.

"Dinner!" Mom called out.

"Saved by the bell!" Annie exclaimed, skipping to the dinning room.

Later in the evening, mom came upstairs to read with Annie, as they had for as many years as either of them could remember.

It had always been their special time, to read, talk, and spend quality time together.

"Mom?" Annie said without turning her head.

"MMhm," Mom murmured into Annie's hair, as she had her cheek pressed to the top of Annie's head.

"Do you remember when you said that you loved me no matter what and that you would never want me to be like everyone else. You said that you liked the fact that I am your unique and interesting little girl. You said that you were happy that my brain is the way it is and you would never want me to be any other way?"

Annie's mom lifted her head looking down into Annie's eyes, "Yes, sweetie, and I meant every word of it."

She hugged her daughter close.

"You said that if the medicine and social skills training could help me to feel happier and to make me feel like I fit in, then you would be very excited to give it a try," Annie squeezed her mom's hand, "Well, I'm really glad we gave it a try."

Annie's mom looked down into her eyes and wrapped her free arm around Annie's shoulders, "Me too, my wonderful girl, me too!"

We hope that you have enjoyed

A Prairie Day with Annie.

Michelle, Josh, and Lili

www.anniebooks.com

www.ingramcontent.com/pod-product-compliance
Lightning Source LLC
Chambersburg PA
CBHW060845280326
41934CB00007B/930